This book belongs to:

____

Made in the USA
Columbia, SC
12 January 2024

30389666R00067